FREDERICK WILLIAMS

Don't Be Scared of AI

A Senior's Guide to Understanding Artificial Intelligence

First edition

This book was professionally typeset on Reedsy.
Find out more at reedsy.com

Contents

1

Introduction

For over a century, science fiction authors have imagined technologies that push the boundaries of what's possible. Jules Verne envisioned space travel in his 1865 novel "From the Earth to the Moon," accurately depicting elements of what would become the Apollo 11 mission just over 100 years later.

Groundbreaking science fiction shows like Star Trek introduced ideas well ahead of their time. The original series featured tractor beams, hyposprays, communicators, and universal translators - concepts that researchers are now working to develop using modern techniques. Lasers and focused sound waves show promise for creating real-life tractor beams. New methods of drug delivery aim to provide needle-free injections like the hypospray. Smartphones have vastly surpassed Star Trek's communicator in functionality with apps for translation and global communication.

The advancement of technology has been made possible by the continuous miniaturization of computer chips. From the use of vacuum tubes in the 1940s to the development of transistors in the 1960s and semiconductor memory and microprocessors in the 1970s, each breakthrough has led to faster and more powerful computers. This has ultimately resulted in the creation of personal computers, smartphones, and tablets in the 1990s and 2000s, as predicted by Moore's Law.

Throughout this evolution, the role of computer hardware and software has been to increase efficiency and productivity. However, with the rise of Artificial Intelligence (AI), the boundaries of what computers can accomplish have been expanded. AI uses algorithms, programs, and data processing tools to perform tasks that previously required human intelligence, such as speech recognition, decision making, pattern and image identification, and problem solving.

For some, this progress may be overwhelming and even frightening, particularly for older adults who may have had limited experience with computers. However, it is important to remember that computers are only as smart as the humans who program them. With proper governance and ethical considerations, AI has the potential to greatly enhance our lives and make tasks easier and more efficient.

2

What scares seniors about AI

The rapid advancements in artificial intelligence (AI) have undoubtedly transformed the way we live, work, and interact with technology. From virtual assistants to self-driving cars, AI has become an integral part of our daily lives. However, while many people are excited about the potential of AI, there is a significant portion of the population who may have reservations or fears about this technology - seniors.

As we age, our familiarity with technology and its advancements may decline, making it challenging to keep up with the rapid pace of AI development. This lack of familiarity and understanding can lead to a sense of fear and apprehension towards AI. In this book, we will delve deeper into each of the reasons why seniors may feel scared or apprehensive about AI and discuss how we can address these concerns to foster a positive perception of AI among seniors.

Reason #1: Lack of Familiarity with Technology and Its Benefits

One of the primary reasons why seniors may feel scared or apprehensive about AI is their lack of familiarity with technology and its potential benefits. Unlike younger generations who have grown up with advanced technology, seniors may not have had the opportunity to learn about AI or understand its potential uses in their lives. This lack of familiarity can lead to a fear of the unknown and skepticism about the usefulness of AI.

To address this, it's essential to provide seniors with accessible resources and training programs that introduce them to AI technology. By demonstrating practical applications and showing how AI can enhance their daily lives, such as voice assistants for reminders or home automation for increased convenience, we can help alleviate their concerns and foster a positive perception of AI.

Reason #2: Concerns about Privacy, Security, and Ethical Issues

Privacy and security are significant concerns for people of all ages, but seniors may be particularly cautious due to their vulnerability to scams or identity theft. They may worry that AI systems could compromise their personal information or invade their privacy. This fear can be heightened by the increasing use of AI in everyday devices, such as smart homes and wearables.

Addressing these concerns involves implementing robust security measures and transparent data handling practices in AI systems. It is crucial to educate seniors about the safeguards in place to protect their privacy and provide them with control over their personal data. Organizations and policymakers should also establish clear ethical guidelines for AI development and use to build trust with seniors and address their concerns about potential misuse of AI technology.

Reason #3: Fear of Losing Control, Autonomy, and Human Connection

Seniors value their independence and the human connection they have with others. They may fear that increasing reliance on AI could erode their sense of control over their lives and reduce opportunities for meaningful human interactions. This fear can be heightened by the growing use of AI in industries such as healthcare, where machines are taking on tasks traditionally performed by humans.

To alleviate these fears, it's important to emphasize that AI is designed to augment human capabilities, not replace them. Highlighting how AI can assist with everyday tasks and improve quality of life can help seniors see it as a tool that empowers them rather than a threat. Additionally, promoting the importance of maintaining social connections and emphasizing the role of AI in facilitating communication and access to information can help seniors embrace technology without feeling isolated.

Reason #4: Perception of AI as a Threat to Their Jobs, Skills, and Social Roles

Seniors who are still in the workforce or seeking employment may worry about AI's impact on job prospects. They may fear that their skills will become obsolete or that AI will replace the need for human workers altogether. This fear can be heightened by the media's portrayal of AI as a job killer.

To address these concerns, it is important to highlight the collaborative nature of human-AI partnerships. Emphasizing the potential for AI to automate repetitive tasks and free up time for more meaningful and complex work can help seniors see it as a complement to their skills rather than a direct threat. Encouraging lifelong learning and providing opportunities for re-skilling or up-skilling can also empower seniors to adapt to changing job market demands and maintain their employability.

Reason #5: Difficulty in Adapting to Rapid Changes and Innovations

The fast-paced nature of technological advancements, including AI, can be challenging for seniors to keep up with. They may feel overwhelmed by the constant updates and struggle to adapt to new technologies. This fear can be heightened by the belief that they may be unable to learn and adapt to new technologies at their age.

To support seniors in adapting to these changes, it is important to provide user-friendly interfaces and intuitive designs that make technology more accessible. Offering training programs specifically tailored to seniors' needs and providing ongoing support can help them feel more comfortable and confident in using AI-based systems. Collaborations between technology companies, community organizations, and senior centers can play a crucial role in bridging the digital divide and ensuring that seniors have the necessary resources to navigate the digital landscape.

Reason #6: Mistrust of the Reliability, Accuracy, and Transparency of AI Systems

Seniors may harbor doubts about the reliability and accuracy of AI systems. They may question the algorithms and data used and worry about potential errors or biases in AI decision-making. This fear can be heightened by the growing use of AI in critical areas, such as healthcare and finance.

To build trust, it is essential to promote transparency in AI systems. This involves providing clear explanations of how AI algorithms work, ensuring accountability for the decisions made by AI systems, and addressing biases and fairness concerns. Independent audits and third-party certifications can also help validate the reliability and accuracy of AI systems, providing seniors with reassurance about their dependability.

Reason #7: Anxiety about the Social and Environmental Impacts of AI

Seniors, like many others, may have concerns about the broader social and environmental consequences of AI. They may worry about job displacement on a larger scale, the potential for AI to amplify existing inequalities, or its impact on the environment. This fear can be heightened by the belief that they may not be able to adapt to the changes brought about by AI.

Addressing these concerns involves fostering responsible AI development and deployment practices. This includes prioritizing fairness, accountability, and transparency in AI systems. It also requires considering the social and environmental implications of AI technologies and working towards minimizing any negative effects. By actively involving seniors in discussions and decision-making processes related to AI policies and regulations, their concerns can be heard and taken into account.

Reason #8: Feeling of Being Left Behind or Excluded by the Digital Divide

Seniors who have limited access to technology or face challenges in using it may feel excluded or left behind. This digital divide can exacerbate their fears of being unable to keep up with rapidly advancing technology, leading to a sense of isolation and fear. This fear can be heightened by the belief that they may not be able to catch up with the younger generation in terms of technology use.

To bridge the digital divide, efforts should be made to ensure affordable and accessible technology for seniors. This can involve initiatives such as providing discounted internet services, offering technology training programs, and establishing community centers where seniors can access and learn about AI technology. Collaborations between technology companies, government agencies, and community organizations can play a crucial role in narrowing the digital divide and ensuring that seniors are not left behind in the digital era.

3

What is AI – (Artificial Intelligence: Fundamental Concepts and Techniques)

A rtificial intelligence has made tremendous progress in recent years, advancing technologies that touch nearly every aspect of our lives. Behind the scenes of these intelligent systems are sophisticated algorithms and techniques that enable machines to mimic human abilities. This chapter provides an overview of some of the core concepts that form the foundation of artificial intelligence.

Understanding these fundamental concepts is important for appreciating how AI is developing rapidly. It also sheds light on the types of challenges researchers are tackling to push the boundaries of machine intelligence. The concepts discussed lay the groundwork for later discussions on specific applications of AI and emerging frontiers in the field.

We will begin with an introduction to artificial intelligence itself and explore machine learning as a key approach that allows systems to improve automatically through experience. Generative AI, computer vision, natural language processing, knowledge representation and reasoning, planning and scheduling, and robotics will then be defined as important subfields that tackle different types of human intelligence.

Artificial intelligence (AI): AI is the ability of machines to mimic human intelligence through tasks like reasoning, learning, problem-solving, and more. Examples include virtual assistants like Siri and chatbots.

Machine learning (ML): ML is a method of AI that allows systems to learn from data and improve over time without being explicitly programmed. Examples include spam filters that learn to detect spam emails and recommender systems that learn user preferences.

Generative AI: Generative AI systems can create new content like images, videos, text or audio based on examples or prompts. Examples include text generators that can write news articles or summaries based on input and GANs (generative adversarial networks) that can generate realistic fake images.

Computer vision: Computer vision is the ability to process and analyze visual images. Examples include self-driving cars that can identify traffic lights and stop signs, facial recognition systems, and medical imaging analysis.

Natural language processing (NLP): NLP allows computers to understand, manipulate and generate human language like text or speech. Examples include machine translation, sentiment analysis, conversational agents, and speech recognition.

Knowledge representation and reasoning: It involves logically representing knowledge and relationships between concepts and then applying logical reasoning techniques to infer new facts. An example is an ontology of medical conditions that can deduce new relationships between diseases.

Planning and scheduling: It involves solving complex constraints and sequencing problems. Examples are package routing by delivery companies, production scheduling in factories, and spacecraft trajectory planning by NASA.

Robotics: Robotics involves developing robots that can complete physical tasks in real-world environments. Examples include industrial robots in factories for material handling, manufacturing and assembly and consumer robots for cleaning (vacuum bots), surgery (surgical robots), and elder assistance.

You should now have a beter understanding of the machine intelligence techniques that power everything from personalized product recommendations to self-driving cars. This computational understanding of intelligence both natural and artificial sets the stage for our continued examination of cutting-edge research and technology. The possibilities of what may be achieved when these concepts advance are only beginning to be revealed.

4

Brief history of AI Major Players – (Top five companies)

In recent years, a number of innovative companies have emerged at the forefront of modern artificial intelligence research and applications. These include both non-profits focused on AI safety as well as for-profit businesses commercializing AI technologies.

OpenAI: Founded in 2015 by Elon Musk and others with a mission to develop artificial general intelligence in a way that is safe and beneficial to humanity. They are a non-profit AI research lab conducting work in areas like language models, robotics, personalized education and more.

Products:

- OpenAI API - Provides programmatic access to AI models like GPT-3 through an API.

- CLIP - A neural network trained on image-text pairs that understands relationships between them.

- DALL-E - An AI model that can generate images from textual prompts.

DeepMind: Founded in 2010 and acquired by Google in 2014, DeepMind is best known for pioneering work in deep learning and training AI systems to master complex games like Go and StarCraft II. Their AlphaGo system defeated top human players in many firsts. DeepMind also does research in areas like protein folding, healthcare and energy efficiency.

Products:

- AlphaGo - AI system that dominated the game of Go, achieving superhuman level play.

- AlphaFold - AI protein structure predictor that has greatly advanced bioinformatics research.

- Flood Forecasting Initiative - Predicts river flooding to help emergency response planning.

Nvidia: Founded in 1993, Nvidia is best known as a manufacturer of graphics processing units (GPUs). However, since the 2010s they have also played a pivotal role in the rise of deep learning by developing GPUs that are especially well-suited to accelerating AI workloads. Their hardware has powered much of the progress made by tech companies and AI research organizations.

Products:

- Graphics processing units (GPUs) - Specialized processors that accelerate deep learning and AI workloads.

- Nvidia DRIVE - Platform for developing self-driving vehicles using Nvidia GPUs, chips and software.

- Nvidia Clara - Healthcare AI platform for medical imaging analysis and drug discovery.

Builder.ai: Founded in 2015, Builder.ai develops AI-powered no-code tools to automate software development and help teams and companies build custom app and web solutions rapidly. Their platform aims to simplify the app creation process and make custom software development more efficient and affordable using AI techniques.

Products:

- Builder Studio - No-code platform to build custom full-stack web and mobile applications.

- Studio Store - Apps marketplace with ready-to-go solutions for common business needs.

- Builder Now - Tool for rapidly prototyping app ideas without coding.

Anthropic: Founded in 2021 under its previous name of "Voxel", Anthropic is an AI safety startup focused on techniques like self-supervised learning to build beneficial AI through advanced computer vision and natural language models. They conduct fundamental research aimed at developing provably beneficial AI that remains helpful, harmless and honest.

Products:

- Constitutional AI Research - Open research on techniques to ensure AI safety like self-supervision.

- PBC Model & API - AI safety model available through an API to other companies for safe deployment.

- Supervised training services - Trains AI models using their techniques to build beneficial systems.

OpenAI and Anthropic are non-profit research labs dedicated to developing advanced AI in a way that benefits humanity. OpenAI created novel systems like GPT-3 and DALL-E, while Anthropic conducts safety-oriented work using techniques like self-supervision.

DeepMind and Nvidia, meanwhile, are leading commercial forces. DeepMind famously achieved superhuman feats in games like Go with AlphaGo, applying deep learning. Nvidia revolutionized AI by designing GPUs that power most deep learning research today.

On the application side, Builder.ai develops AI-powered no-code tools that allow organizations to build their own custom software rapidly. Their platform automates app development using AI.

Together, these companies represent both the theoretical and practical progress being made at the cutting edge of AI. From pioneering deep learning to commercializing its applications, to researching how to ensure advanced AI remains safe and beneficial as it continues to develop, they offer a glimpse into both the promise and responsibility that comes with developing increasingly powerful technologies. Their innovative work is pushing the boundaries of what is possible with artificial intelligence.

5

AI tools that can aid in senior living and learning

E xpanding on the topic of AI tools that can aid in senior living and learning, there are numerous technological advancements that are specifically designed to improve the quality of life for older adults. These tools range from smart home devices to virtual reality devices, and they all have the potential to make daily tasks and activities easier for seniors, as well as provide opportunities for continued learning and social interaction.

One of the most popular and widely used AI tools for seniors is smart home devices. These devices, such as Amazon Echo or Google Nest, can be controlled through voice commands and can assist with a variety of tasks. For seniors, this can mean controlling lights, thermostats, and appliances without needing to get up or move around. These devices can also be connected to other smart devices in the home, such as security systems and medication reminders, providing a safer and more convenient living environment.

Another AI tool that has become increasingly popular in recent years is voice assistants. These are virtual assistants that can be accessed through smart devices or smartphones, and can perform tasks and provide information through voice commands. For seniors, these assistants can help with scheduling appointments, setting reminders, and even ordering groceries or medication. They can also provide companionship and entertainment, as they are designed to respond to conversation and engage in small talk.

Wearable devices are another AI tool that has great potential for seniors. These devices, such as smartwatches or fitness trackers, can monitor health and fitness levels, track daily activities, and provide alerts for potential health issues. For seniors who may have health concerns or mobility limitations, these devices can be lifesaving. They can also provide motivation for staying active and healthy, as they can track progress and set goals.

Online platforms and virtual reality devices are also valuable AI tools for seniors. These platforms and devices can provide access to a wide range of information and resources, such as online classes, virtual tours, and social networking sites. This allows seniors to continue learning and exploring new interests, even if they are unable to leave their home. It also provides opportunities for social interaction and staying connected with loved ones, which is crucial for mental and emotional well-being.

In addition to virtual reality devices, there are also robotic companions that can provide similar benefits for seniors. These robots, such as Paro or Buddy, are designed to provide companionship and assistance with daily tasks. They can also monitor health and provide reminders for medication or appointments. For seniors who may live alone or have limited social interaction, these robots can provide a sense of companionship and reduce feelings of isolation.

Telemedicine devices are another important AI tool for seniors, especially in the current global health crisis. These devices, such as remote monitoring systems or video conferencing platforms, enable seniors to receive medical care and consultations from the comfort of their own home. This can be especially beneficial for seniors with chronic health conditions or mobility limitations, as it eliminates the need for frequent trips to the doctor's office.

Smart speakers, such as Amazon Echo or Google Home, are also becoming increasingly popular among seniors. These devices can provide a range of benefits, from playing music and audiobooks to providing reminders and information. They can also be connected to other smart devices in the home, making it easier for seniors to control their environment and stay connected.

Lastly, image recognition apps are a crucial AI tool for seniors who may have difficulty with vision or memory. These apps can scan and recognize objects, helping seniors to identify items and keep track of their belongings. They can also be used to organize and label photos and documents, making it easier for seniors to access and reminisce on past memories.

Overall, AI tools have the potential to greatly improve the quality of life for seniors. These technologies can assist with daily tasks, provide companionship and entertainment, and promote continued learning and social interaction. As technology continues to advance, it is important for these tools to be accessible and user-friendly for seniors, allowing them to fully benefit from the advantages they offer. With the growing aging population, incorporating AI tools into senior living and learning is essential for promoting independence, health, and well-being.

6

Issues and concerns

Ethical and moral dilemmas surrounding the use of AI in senior living and learning are a growing concern. As AI becomes more integrated into our daily lives, questions arise about how it should be used and who is responsible for its actions. One major ethical dilemma is the potential for AI to replace human caregivers in the elder care industry. While AI tools can provide assistance and companionship, they cannot replace the emotional connection and empathy that a human caregiver can provide. This raises questions about the moral implications of relying on AI for senior care and the potential for dehumanization.

One potential solution to address these ethical and moral dilemmas is to involve seniors in the development and testing of AI tools. By including their perspectives and feedback, developers can better understand the needs and concerns of the senior population and create more tailored and user-friendly tools. This can also help mitigate any potential issues with dehumanization, as seniors can provide valuable insight into how AI can be used to enhance, rather than replace, human care.

Social and economic impacts of AI in senior living and learning are also important to consider. On one hand, AI tools can improve the quality of life for seniors by providing assistance and opportunities for continued learning and social interaction. However, there is also concern that these tools may widen the digital divide between technologically literate seniors and those who are not as tech-savvy. This could further isolate certain groups of seniors and limit their access to the benefits of AI. Additionally, the cost of implementing and maintaining AI tools may also create socioeconomic disparities, as not all seniors may have the financial means to access these technologies.

In terms of social and economic impacts, it is important for there to be efforts to bridge the digital divide and ensure equal access to AI tools for all seniors. This may include providing training and support for seniors who are not as familiar with technology, as well as finding ways to make these tools more affordable and accessible for those with lower incomes.

Accountability and transparency are crucial when it comes to the use of AI in senior living and learning. As AI becomes more integrated into our daily lives, it is important for there to be clear guidelines and protocols for its use. This includes transparency in how data is collected, stored, and used by AI tools, as well as accountability for any errors or malfunctions. For example, if a telemedicine device fails to properly monitor a senior's health, who is responsible for the consequences? It is important for the developers and manufacturers of AI tools to be held accountable for their products and for there to be transparency in how these tools operate.

Accountability and transparency can be achieved through clear regulations and guidelines for the use of AI in senior living and learning. This may also include implementing ethical standards and codes of conduct for AI developers and manufacturers to follow. Regular evaluations and audits can also help ensure compliance and identify any issues that need to be addressed.

Safety and reliability are also major concerns when it comes to AI tools for seniors. These tools must be designed and tested rigorously to ensure they are safe and reliable for use by older adults. For example, if a robotic companion malfunctions and causes harm to a senior, this could have serious consequences. Additionally, AI tools must be regularly updated and maintained to ensure their reliability. Seniors must be able to trust that the AI tools they are using will perform as intended and not put their safety at risk.

To ensure safety and reliability, it is crucial for AI tools to undergo thorough testing and quality control measures before being released to the market. Ongoing monitoring and updates can also help address any potential issues that may arise. Additionally, there should be clear protocols in place for reporting and addressing any malfunctions or safety concerns.

Governance and regulation of AI in senior living and learning is also an important consideration. As the use of AI in this field continues to grow, there needs to be clear guidelines and regulations in place to ensure its ethical and responsible use. This may include regulations around data privacy, accountability, and safety standards. It is also important for there to be collaboration between government agencies, AI developers, and senior care organizations to establish effective governance and regulation for this rapidly advancing technology.

Finally, effective governance and regulation of AI in senior living and learning will require collaboration and communication between various stakeholders, including government agencies, AI developers, and senior care organizations. By working together, they can establish guidelines and standards that promote the responsible and ethical use of AI for the benefit of seniors.

While AI tools offer many potential benefits for seniors in terms of living and learning, there are also important ethical, social, economic, and regulatory considerations that must be addressed. It is crucial for these tools to be developed and implemented responsibly, with the well-being of seniors at the forefront. As AI technology continues to advance, it is essential for these concerns to be addressed and for there to be ongoing evaluation and improvement to ensure the safe and ethical use of AI in senior living and learning.

7

Conclusion:

Artificial intelligence (AI) is a rapidly evolving field that encompasses a variety of technologies such as machine learning, computer vision, and natural language processing. These technologies have the potential to revolutionize industries and improve our daily lives in countless ways. However, as with any powerful tool, there are also concerns and ethical considerations that must be addressed.

Forging AI development, AI has been dominated by major players such as OpenAI, DeepMind, Nvidia, Builder.ai, and Anthropic (Voxel). These companies have made significant contributions to the field and continue to push the boundaries of what is possible with AI.

In terms of senior living and learning, AI tools such as smart home devices, voice assistants, and wearable devices can greatly aid in improving the quality of life for seniors. These technologies can help with daily tasks, monitoring health, and staying connected with loved ones.

However, with the rapid advancement of AI, there are also concerns about its potential impact on society. Issues such as ethical and moral dilemmas, social and economic impacts, and accountability and transparency must be carefully considered and addressed. Proper governance and regulation are also necessary to ensure the responsible and safe development and use of AI.

AI has the potential to bring about significant positive change, but it must be approached with caution and responsibility. As we continue to explore the possibilities of AI, it is important to prioritize ethical considerations and ensure that its development benefits society as a whole.

If you found this book helpful, I'd appreciate if you left a favorable review for the book on Amazon.

8

Available Resources for Seniors:

1. **AARP** - The American Association of Retired Persons offers resources and information for seniors on a variety of topics, including technology and AI.

2. **Senior Planet** - An online community and resource center for seniors interested in technology and digital literacy.

3. **National Council on Aging** - Provides resources and support for seniors to stay connected and informed about technology.

4. **TechBoomers** - A website that offers free online courses and tutorials for seniors on a variety of technology topics, including AI.

5. **SeniorNet** - An organization that offers classes and resources specifically for seniors to learn about technology and stay connected.

6. **Older Adults Technology Services** - Provides training and support for seniors to learn about and use technology, including AI.

7. **SeniorNet Learning Center** - A website that offers online classes and resources for seniors to learn about technology and AI.

8. **SeniorTech** - An online magazine and resource center for older adults to stay informed about technology and AI.

9. **National Institute on Aging** - Offers resources and information for

seniors on a variety of topics, including technology and AI.

10. **Local community centers and libraries** - Many local community centers and libraries offer classes and workshops for seniors to learn about technology and AI.

9

Resources:

Science fact: Sci-fi inventions that became reality - BBC News
BBC News. (2016, November 18). Science fact: Sci-fi
inventions that became reality.
BBC News. https://www.bbc.com/news/health-38026393

Welcome to the future: 11 ideas that went from science fiction to reality
| Space
Cavendish, L., & Magazine, A. a. S. (2020, March 25). *Welcome to
the future: 11 ideas that went from science fiction to reality.* Space.com.
https://www.space.com/science-fiction-turned-reality.html

Then and Now: How 30 Years of Progress Have Changed PCs | TechSpot
Evanson, N. (2023, June 27). *Then and Now: How 30 years of progress
have changed PCs.* TechSpot. https://www.techspot.com/article/2693-3
0-years-of-pc-progress/

Student-Guide-Module-1-Fundamentals-of-AI.pdf (microsoft.com)
Fundamentals of Artificial Intelligence. (n.d.). *news.microsoft.com/wp-*

RESOURCES:

content/uploads/prod/sites/93/2020/04/Student-Guide-Module-1-Fundamentals-of-AI.pdf. Retrieved January 24, 2024, from https://news.microsoft.com/wp-content/uploads/prod/sites/93/2020/04/Student-Guide-Module-1-Fundamentals-of-AI.pdf

www.ingramcontent.com/pod-product-compliance
Lightning Source LLC
LaVergne TN
LVHW022127060326
832903LV00063B/4797